D1530759

PEOPLE OF CHARACTER

John F. Kennedy

A Life of Citizenship

Written by Anne Todd
Illustrated by Tina Walski

BLASTOFF!
4
READERS

BELLWETHER MEDIA • MINNEAPOLIS, MN

Note to Librarians, Teachers, and Parents:

Blastoff! Readers are carefully developed by literacy experts and combine standards-based content with developmentally-appropriate text.

Level 1 provides the most support through repetition of high-frequency words, light text, predictable sentence patterns, and strong visual support.

Level 2 offers early readers a bit more challenge through varied simple sentences, increased text load, and less repetition of high frequency words.

Level 3 advances early-fluent readers toward fluency through increased text and concept load, less reliance on visuals, longer sentences, and more literary language.

Level 4 builds reading stamina by providing more text per page, increased use of punctuation, greater variation in sentence patterns, and increasingly challenging vocabulary.

Level 5 encourages children to move from "learning to read" to "reading to learn" by providing even more text, varied writing styles, and less familiar topics.

Whichever book is right for your reader, Blastoff! Readers are the perfect books to build confidence and encourage a love of reading that will last a lifetime!

This edition first published in 2008 by Bellwether Media.

No part of this publication may be reproduced in whole or in part without written permission of the publisher. For information regarding permission, write to Bellwether Media Inc., Attention: Permissions Department, Post Office Box 1C, Minnetonka, MN 55345-9998.

Library of Congress Cataloging-in-Publication Data
Todd, Anne.
  John F. Kennedy : a life of citizenship / by Anne Todd.
    p. cm. – (Blastoff! readers : people of character)
Summary: "People of character explores the important character traits through the lives of famous hisotrical figures. John F. Kennedy highlights how this great individual demonstrated citizenship during his life. Intended for grades three through six"—Provided by publisher.
  Includes bibliographical references and index.
  ISBN-13: 978-1-60014-087-7 (hardcover : alk. paper)
  ISBN-10: 1-60014-087-4 (hardcover : alk. paper)
  1. Kennedy, John F. (John Fitzgerald), 1917–1963–Juvenile Title.

E842.Z9T63 2008
973.922092–dc22
  [B]   2007021047

Contents

Meet John F. Kennedy 4

Helping Others 9

The Thirty-fifth President 13

Good Citizenship 15

Glossary 22

To Learn More 23

Index 24

Who is responsible for your community? John F. Kennedy would say you are responsible. He was the 35th President of the United States. John believed being a **citizen** means more than just belonging to a community. He believed good citizens should try to help their community.

John was born in 1917 to a wealthy family in Massachusetts. He was one of nine children. When he was young, he liked to travel and play sports.

He was also popular and smart. He attended many good schools, including a highly respected college called Harvard.

After college, John joined the U.S Navy. He served on a ship during **World War II**. One day an enemy ship struck his ship. Some crew members had to jump into the water to survive. Several people were injured, including John.

Still, John led the survivors to shore.
John even pulled along another man
who was too injured to swim.
John believed people should always
work together and help each other.

After the war, John decided to enter **politics**. He wanted to work for change in his community. At that time, African-Americans were treated unfairly. They could not go to the same schools as white people.

Schools for black children were not as good as schools for white children. There were laws that kept white and black people separate in other ways too. John worked to promote **equal rights** for all people.

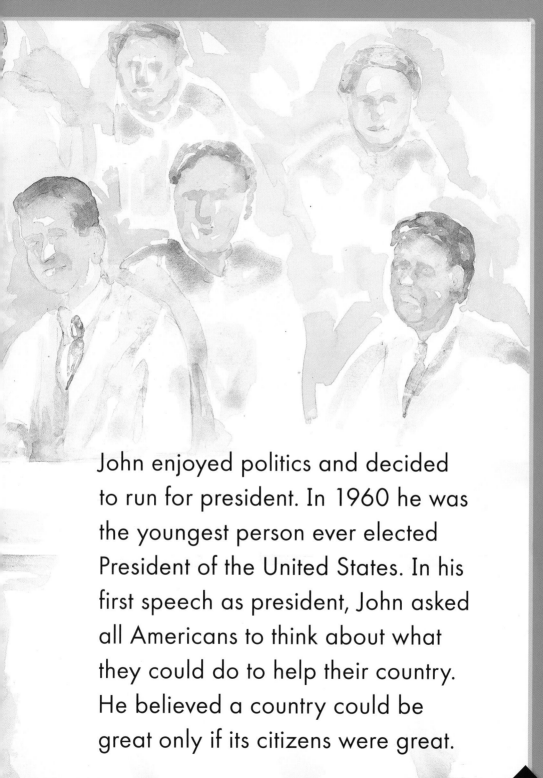

John enjoyed politics and decided to run for president. In 1960 he was the youngest person ever elected President of the United States. In his first speech as president, John asked all Americans to think about what they could do to help their country. He believed a country could be great only if its citizens were great.

John felt that being a good citizen meant helping others in need. That's why he started the **Peace Corps**. This group let Americans volunteer all over the world. American volunteers went to communities that needed help. Volunteers would teach people, plant crops, build houses, and help communities grow.

John wanted Americans
to work hard in school.
He knew the importance
of education and that
learning could lead
to new discoveries.
John especially wanted
Americans to lead the world
in space exploration.
He wanted the United
States to be the first to land
a person on the moon.
This space race motivated
many students to work
hard studying science.

John **inspired** many people to help others and work harder for their community. He brought change to the country, but some people worried that things were changing too fast. In 1963, John was shot and killed. It was a sad day for America.

Even so, the people who believed in John stayed strong and continued the work he had started.

After John's death, an American
landed on the moon. The Peace
Corps continued to grow.
Americans still volunteered in their
communities and around the world.

There is still work to be done. John would say we are all responsible for helping our communities and our country. What could you do to help your community?

Glossary

citizen—a person who is a member of a country or state

equal rights—the state of being treated equally under the law

inspired—made people want to do something by showing them a good example

Peace Corps—an American organization that sends volunteers all over the world to help people in need

politics—the activity and debate in governing a state or country

World War II—a war that started in Europe in 1939 that spread to many other parts of the globe; World War II ended in 1945.

To Learn More

AT THE LIBRARY

Hodge, Marie. *John F. Kennedy: Voice of Hope*. New York: Sterling, 2007.

Jones, Veda Boyd. *John F. Kennedy*. New York: Children's Press, 2006.

Riehecky, Janet. *Citizenship*. Mankato, Minn.: Capstone, 2007.

ON THE WEB

Learning more about John F. Kennedy is as easy as 1, 2, 3.

1. Go to www.factsurfer.com

2. Enter "John F. Kennedy" into search box.

3. Click the "Surf" button and you will see a list of related web sites.

With factsurfer.com, finding more information is just a click away.

Index

1917, 6
1960, 13
1963, 18
African-Americans, 10
America, 18
American, 13, 15, 16, 20
citizenship, 5, 13, 15
community, 5, 10, 15, 18, 20, 21
discoveries, 16
equal rights, 11
Harvard, 7
Massachusetts, 6
moon, 16, 20
Peace Corps, 15, 20
politics, 10, 13
President of the United States, 5, 13
science, 16
space, 16
U.S. Navy, 8
volunteers, 15, 20
World War II, 8, 10